15   Aldwych
Fleet Street
St Paul's Cathedral

TOWER HILL

WLT 871

L IS FOR LONDON

PAUL THURLBY

For Ely, my armchair art editor.
With special thanks to Emma and
Izzy at Hodder for helping me to
make this book. How about Paris
and New York next?

HODDER CHILDREN'S BOOKS
First published in Great Britain in 2015 by Hodder and Stoughton
This paperback edition published in 2016

A CIP catalogue record for this book is available from the British Library.

ISBN: 978 1 444 91878 6

10 9 8 7 6 5 4 3 2 1

Printed and bound in China

Hodder Children's Books
An imprint of Hachette Children's Group
Part of Hodder and Stoughton
Carmelite House
50 Victoria Embankment
London EC4Y 0DZ

An Hachette UK Company
www.hachette.co.uk
www.hachettechildrens.co.uk

L IS FOR LONDON

PAUL THURLBY

Hodder
Children's
Books

ABBEY ROAD

attracts thousands of tourists each year to its zebra crossing, trying to recreate the Beatles' famous Abbey Road album cover.

Paul   John   Ringo   George

ABBEY ROAD

BOROUGH MARKET

is one of the oldest and largest food markets in London. It is thought to have been around for over 1000 years.

NEW SEASON

Grouse
Partridge
Pigeon
Wild ducks
Lakeland rabbits
Lakeland hares
Lakeland pheasant

World Famous
'Ultra Chocolate Brownie'
£1.50

DON'T KNOCK!

ORGANIC FRENCH BAGUETTES
£1.30

CABS in London are famous for being black. If you hail one you can be sure that your driver will know the quickest route to your destination without needing a satnav.

↑

Drivers must pass
'The Knowledge',
a demanding test of
London's back streets
and landmarks.

When they need a break, cabbies can stop at one of 13 cab shelters scattered around London for a nice cup of tea.

CAB

Downing Street

is one of the most famous streets in the world.
The Prime Minister lives at Number 10.

The famous black brickwork is the result of pollution. It was originally yellow.

Larry is the chief mouser at Number 10.

DOWNING
STREET SW1

The 32 capsules on the London Eye represent the 32 London boroughs.

ENFIELD
BARNET
WALTHAM FOREST
HARROW
HARINGEY
REDBRIDGE
HAVERING
HILLINGDON
BRENT
CAMDEN
ISLINGTON
HACKNEY
NEWHAM
BARKING & DAGENHAM
TOWER HAMLETS
CITY
WESTMINSTER
KENSINGTON & CHELSEA
HAMMERSMITH & FULHAM
EALING
SOUTHWARK
GREENWICH
BEXLEY
HOUNSLOW
LAMBETH
WANDSWORTH
RICHMOND
LEWISHAM
MERTON
KINGSTON
BROMLEY
SUTTON
CROYDON

THE LONDON EYE

is the world's largest observation wheel.

On the other side of the River Thames from the London Eye are the Houses of Parliament. The clock tower, better known as 'Big Ben', is one of the top London attractions.

FOYLES

is one of London's most famous bookshops.

Its flagship store on Charing Cross Road holds up to 800,000 books.

HUMOUR

SCIENCE & MATHEMATICS

FICTION & POETRY

FILM, TV & DRAMA

LANGUAGES

CHILDREN'S

SPORT & HOBBIES

TRAVEL & MAPS

ARCHITECTURE & DESIGN

HISTORY

BUSINESS

FOOD & DRINK

ART, FASHION & PHOTOGRAPHY

This is just a selection!

THE GLOBE

was originally built in 1599, and twice rebuilt. When the theatre was rebuilt in the 1990s, special permission was granted to have a thatched roof as these had been banned after the Great Fire of London in 1666.

Born in Stratford-upon-Avon in 1564, William Shakespeare is widely considered to be the greatest writer of all time.

Shakespeare's

Globe

HARRODS

is an upmarket department store in Knightsbridge. It is the biggest in Europe and welcomes up to 300,000 visitors a day.

The shop's 330 departments include the Egyptian Room.

ICE SKATING

has become a festive tradition in London at Christmas time. Every winter Somerset House, originally a palace, is transformed into a traditional outdoor ice rink.

This experience is open day and night, when the ice comes alive with music.

Ice Skating

THE CROWN JEWELS

are displayed to millions of visitors every year, guarded
by the Beefeaters in the Tower of London.
The Imperial State Crown is the most famous crown
in the world. It's set with over 3,000 gems.

The Crown Jewels are still
used by the Queen in important
national ceremonies.

KEW GARDENS

is one of the world's most important botanical gardens and home to the largest collection of living plants in the world. There are over 50,000 different species to discover!

The treetop walkway is one of the most popular attractions at Kew. The platform is 18 metres (59 feet) above the ground.

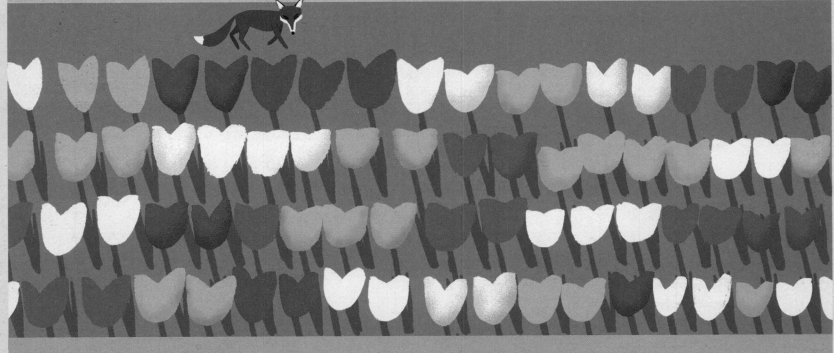

KEW GARDENS

THE LONDON BUS

is one of London's main icons. Although the original Routemaster bus has largely been phased out, buses in London are still red and remain a recognised symbol of the city.

15 Aldwych Fleet Street St Paul's Cathedral

TOWER HILL

WLT 871

It takes around 55 hours of training for a bus driver to become fully qualified.

MILLENNIUM BRIDGE

is nicknamed the 'wobbly bridge' after it swayed from side to side on its opening day. The southern end of the bridge is near the Tate Modern and the northern end is near St Paul's Cathedral.

Originally a power station, the Tate Modern is London's museum of modern art and one of the world's most visited galleries.

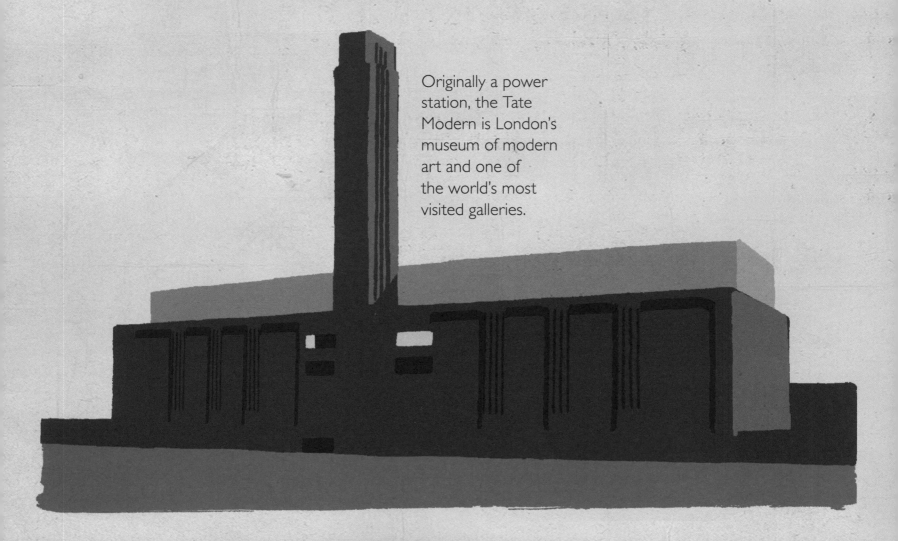

MILLENNIUM BRIDGE

NELSON'S COLUMN

rises above the surrounding buildings in Trafalgar Square. Lord Nelson was an officer in the Royal Navy and was noted for his leadership which led him to many victories.

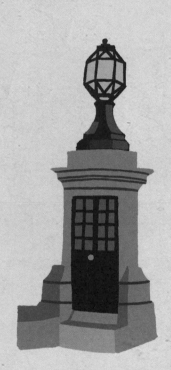

Also in Trafalgar Square, you'll find the National Gallery and the world's smallest police station.

Lord Nelson lost his arm in battle.

Nelson's Column

THE OLYMPIC PARK

was built for the 2012 Summer Olympics and
Paralympics. It contains the Olympic Stadium
and London Aquatics Centre, amongst
other venues.

The park is overlooked by the Orbit, designed by Anish
Kapoor, which is Britain's largest piece of public art.

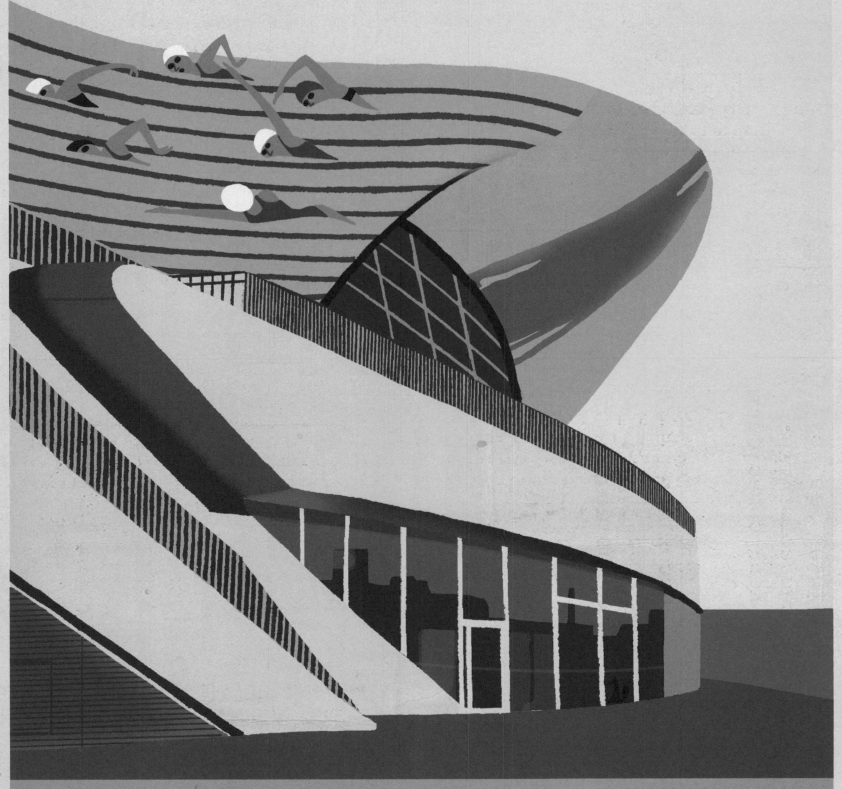

OLYMPIC PARK

PARKS are the lungs of London. There are eight Royal Parks in central London, covering over 5000 acres.

In Hyde Park, you can go horse riding along 'Rotten Row'.

Park Life

Britons spend six months of their lives queuing.

ROYAL GUARDS

are the men you see standing
very still in front of
Buckingham Palace.

The Guards are highly
trained combat soldiers
and are known for not
smiling while on duty.

ROYAL GUARDS

St Pancras

International railway station is one of the biggest and best-loved landmarks in London. It serves as a gateway to Europe.

The Eurostar trains run through the Channel Tunnel under the sea between Great Britain and France.

ST PANCRAS

TOWER BRIDGE

was built between 1886 and 1894.
It is situated near the Tower of
London. According to legend,
a wealthy American bought the
old London Bridge thinking
it was Tower Bridge.

There is now a glass walkway which offers a view
of London life 42 metres above the River Thames.

TOWER
BRIDGE

THE UNDERGROUND

is the oldest underground railway in the world.
It is known as 'the Tube' due to the shape
of its tunnels.

The deepest line is the Northen Line at Hampstead where the trains run 58.5 metres under ground.

1 Elephant & Castle 5mins
2 Elephant & Castle 8mins
09:45:16
← Way Out
← Northern Line
← Waterloo & City Line
← Way Out
Waterloo
Elephant & Castle
UNDERGROUND

V&A MUSEUM

is the world's largest museum of
decorative arts and design with a
collection of over 4.5 million objects. It was
named after Queen Victoria (1819–1901)
and Prince Albert (1819–1861).

Tipu's Tiger, a lifesize wooden carving, is one
of the museum's most famous exhibits.

V&A MUSEUM

Wimbledon is the oldest and biggest tennis tournament in the world and the only Grand Slam to be played on grass.

There is a strict dress code in operation. Players must wear white clothing.

WIMBLEDON

oXo TOWER

was originally constructed as a power station. It now contains a restaurant, galleries and shops.

Further along the South Bank, you will find a popular skate-boarding park and the Royal Festival Hall, part of the Southbank Centre.

ROYAL FESTIVAL HALL

The Royal Festival Hall is one of the most popular arts venues in Britain.

OXO TOWER

Yeoman Warders

guard the Tower of London. Their nickname is 'Beefeaters'. Legend says that if the ravens ever leave the Tower, Britain will fall.

In 2014, to commemorate the centenary of the outbreak of World War I, 888,246 ceramic poppies were installed to represent each of the fallen soldiers.

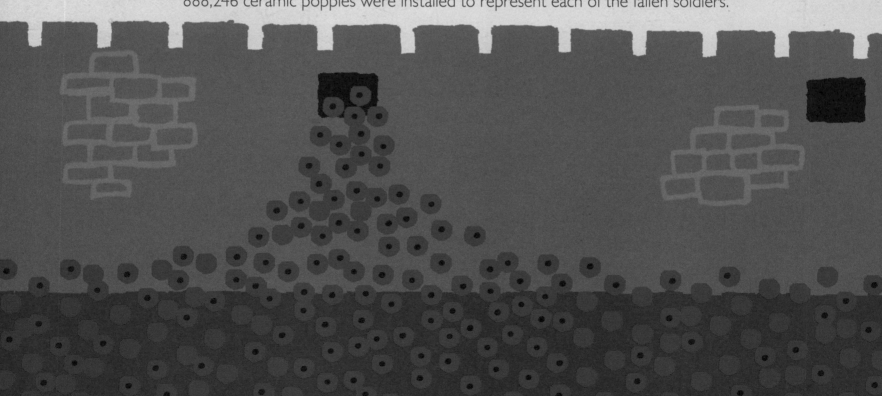

YEOMAN

LONDON ZOO

is the world's oldest scientific zoo. Today it houses a collection of over 750 species of animals.

The giraffe enclosure is always a favourite with visitors.

One of my lifelong ambitions had been to illustrate my own book about London, the city I call home. For me, using the alphabet is a way of structuring the book. From there, I expand on each illustration and tell the reader a little more about the famous landmarks and amazing sights.

Whilst working on this book I discovered, to my surprise, that in the 1960s St Pancras Station was due to be demolished in the name of modernisation. Thankfully that never happened and it is now one of London's most iconic buildings. Preserving the character of the city is very important if we want it to remain unique.

By the way, it sometimes rains in London.

Did you spot the sneaky fox in each spread? Foxes have made London their home.

Originally from Nottingham, now based in London, I have been a full-time illustrator since September 2006.

I'd like to thank my junior school teachers for seeing that I could draw and write, despite holding my pen differently, and for recognising that there is no set way of doing things.

I've built up an impressive list of commissions working in editorial, advertising, design, publishing and T-shirt design for clients including the *Guardian,* the *New Yorker,* The French Tourist Board, Templar Publishing, Ted Baker, It's Nice That, Pimm's and The Southbank Centre, London.

Winning the Bologna Ragazzi Opera Prima Award in 2013 for my first book, ALPHABET, was one of the proudest achievements of my career so far.

Paul Thurlby

BEAUTIFUL BOOKS
BY PAUL THURLBY:

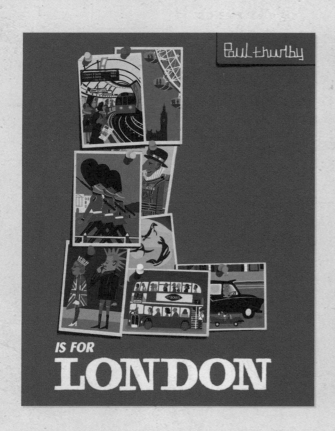

For fun activities, further
information and to order, visit
www.hodderchildrens.co.uk